Caution: Do Not Read This Book

Caution: Do Not Read This Book

Edited by Holly Winter
Winuply Press
New York

Caution: Do Not Read This Book

Winuply Press
Caution: Do Not Read This Book
Editor: Holly Winter
New York
Copyright © 2017
All Rights Reserved

Read this book and enjoy it. Please don't copy anything. If you copy anything, pig guts will be smeared on your hair. Eggs will be poured into your socks and mud will be poured into your shoes. We will draw a mustache and a unibrow on your face. We will shave your head. Just kidding. DO NOT COPY OUR BOOK! Please!

Chief Encouragers: Sharon Huppert, Holly Winter Huppert
Copy Editor: Betsy Osgood
Cover Design: Joselin, Opal, Kenya, Aurora, Lisbeth, Nevaeh, Piper, Carlos
Front Cover Clues: Joselin, Opal, Kenya, Aurora, Lisbeth, Nevaeh, Piper
Back Cover Copy: Kenya and Opal
Interior Placement: Sharon Huppert, Holly Winter
Interior Design: Joselin, Opal, Kenya, Massiel, Carlos, Victor, Aurora, Lisbeth, Johnny, Katherine, Nevaeh, Manuel, Piper

Caution: Do Not Read This Book

Contents

Introduction 1

Stories..5

Piper: Lost 7

Johnny: Stuck with a Hurt Pinky 13

Joselin: The Story of a Tooth 19

Fred: Running into Things 23

Nevaeh: Hissy Fits 27

Jorge: About Soccer..33

Aurora: Oaxaca, Mexico 37

Manny: I Love the Snow 43

Katherine: Scared at the Mall 47

Carlos: Visiting my Cousins 51

Massiel: I Love Chocolate 55

Victor: The Wrong Store 59

Heavenlee: Gymnastics 63

Caution: Do Not Read This Book

Lisbeth: Sea Adventure 67

Toby: LEGOs 73

Opal: What I Imagine When I'm Bored 77

Kenya: Jamaica 81

Acknowledgements: 89

Biographies 91

Afterward: The Game of Writing 113

Thank You! 118

Caution: Do Not Read This Book

Caution: Do Not Read This Book

Caution: Do Not Read This Book

Introduction

THE BOOK, <u>Caution: Do Not Read This Book</u> was written by children at the George Washington (public) Montessori School in Kingston, NY. Some third- and fourth-graders came to school early on Wednesdays and Fridays to work on this book. We got here at 7:30 in the morning. That is an early time for children to come to school, because we need our sleep.

Writing this book was both frustrating and fun. It was hard because you had to get your writing pretty perfect. If there was a mistake, we would cross it out and rewrite the mistake. Our papers were messy with all of our changes, but in the end our stories were better. We knew our stories would be more interesting and have more grit if we made them better and better.

We wrote about many different ideas. Opal wrote about what she thinks about when she's bored. You're going to want to read this one. Kenya wrote about a trip she took with her mother to Jamaica. Warning: This story might make you hungry.

Seventeen students wrote this book. Be prepared for seventeen amazing stories. There are many emotions in this book. The reader might feel scared, excited, sad or even curious when reading these stories.

Our book is on sale at www.amazon.com.

Please write good reviews on <u>Caution: Do Not Read This Book</u> because we worked very hard. We put all of our concentration and our hearts into this book.

We know the title is, "Caution: Do Not Read This Book." We actually do want you to read the book. We called it that to make it seem like a fun book. Children like to be funny.

Caution: Do Not Read This Book

We want people to know that we accomplished something very hard. Children can do things like adults can do.

Thank you for buying and reading this book.

By Kenya, 3rd Grade
By Opal, 3rd Grade

Caution: Do Not Read This Book

Caution: Do Not Read This Book

Stories

Caution: Do Not Read This Book

Piper: Lost

I REMEMBER. It was the afternoon. My family and I were all getting ready to go to Grandma's house. Mom was packing clothes. My dad just got home from work and he had to shave. Penny and I were ready to go. We were playing tag outside. I was "it" and Penny was running away from me and went into the bushes, because she thought I wouldn't be able to see her. I could see her. When she saw that I could see her, she ran the other way. I chased her.

My mom and dad came out of the house. My dad was carrying the suitcase and my mom was carrying the overnight bag. Mom said, "All right. It's time to go." Dad was walking towards the car. He looked around the yard and said, "Where's your brother?"

Penny said, "I don't know."

I looked around the yard and said, "He wasn't with us."

Mom looked at me. I said, "I thought he was with you."

Fletcher was 5 years old at the time. I was 7 and Penny was 3. Usually Fletcher didn't go out of sight; he stayed near us. If we were walking, he might go up ahead a little. Normally we could see him very easily. He wasn't usually missing.

We looked around the yard. I noticed the gate that leads to the road and the driveway was open. It scared me. Did he run off? Did he leave the yard? He had never left the yard by himself before, but now he was gone.

I didn't want to yell to my parents and tell them that the gate was open because I didn't want to freak them out. Penny yelled it.

Mom and Dad had frightened looks on their faces. Mom wasn't smiling and her eyes were big. It looked like Dad stopped breathing, but he didn't really. Mom and Dad both said we need to look around outside. Dad put the suitcase into the car while Mom looked out the gate towards the street.

Where is he? Is he out there?

We went down the street to look down the second street. We couldn't see him. My heart was beating really fast. I thought to myself, "Oh my God. What's happening?"

We went back to the house to search inside. We split up. Penny and I went upstairs to search for him, Mom and Dad stayed downstairs. He wasn't in the house.

Where is he? Is he outside?

We went outside and searched the yard again. We looked at the end of the yard and at the very beginning of the yard. We searched under the porch. We looked in the sandbox and under the slide. He wasn't there.

Penny and I went back inside to look some more. Mom and Dad searched the garage. Just as Penny and I were about to go outside, we heard something coming from the closet in the front hall. I thought to myself, "What's in there?" I was making up stories in my head because I was all scared inside. "Is it an animal?"

Penny and I screamed when we heard the noise again. Penny went to the door and put her hand on the doorknob. She opened the door. We couldn't see anything. We had already looked in the closet and nothing was there. We saw the coats starting to move. I was scared. I thought to myself, "What's in there? Oh my God!"

All of a sudden, something came out of the closet. We had no idea what it was because it moved so fast. Then we saw what it was. It was Fletcher.

Fletcher was smiling like this was a fun game he was playing.

Caution: Do Not Read This Book

I was annoyed. "You didn't tell me we were playing hide and seek."

My parents came in the house. They asked Penny and me to go in the other room. They were mad that he was hiding but happy that we found him. Fletcher had to have a long talk about it with my parents. I don't know what they said, but they talked to him a long time, it felt like a half hour.

We still went to Grandma's. Fletcher sat in the car smiling because he didn't understand that he did something bad. Mom and Dad drove but didn't talk. Penny and I were in the back seat with our dolls.

I was kind of tired from all the worrying, but I was ready to have fun playing with my dolls.

Caution: Do Not Read This Book

Caution: Do Not Read This Book

Johnny: Stuck with a Hurt Pinky

ONE TIME I WENT TO INTRAMURALS and I was so excited because I like to play sports. We were playing Tiger Ball, which is a mixture of basketball and soccer. You use a soccer ball. You can kick the ball or bounce it with your hands and score with your hands. But you can only grab the ball when it's over your knees. I scored two goals. My team was winning. I was happy because I don't like to lose.

At the end of the game, I had the ball and I was trying to get past someone. Since the gym was so small, when I tried getting past that kid, I hurt myself. Someone rushed past and squished my hand. I closed my eyes and saw red. I tried to move my pinky and it hurt bad. You know when you wiggle something and you think the pain will go away? That's what I thought. I thought the pain would go away. It didn't.

It hurt. Bad. I went to tell Coach that I hurt myself. He told me to wiggle my pinky for him. You know when someone knows you have a sprained ankle and they say, "Get over it"? That's how I felt when Coach told me to wiggle my finger. I already wiggled my finger and now he wanted me to do it again? I had to wiggle it in front of him. It hurt.

I went to my classroom and told my teachers that I hurt my hand. They told me to go to the nurse for her to check it. The nurse listened to what I said and then looked at my hand. She told me to move it. I didn't mind when she asked me to move it, because she's a nurse. I get it. I moved my pinky. Bad things happened. It hurt. She told me my pinky might be sprained. I knew that meant it might have twisted or something. I wasn't worried,

Caution: Do Not Read This Book

because my cousins have done this before and I knew how to get it treated.

My cousin's mom had a daughter who sprained her foot. I watched how her daughter got her treatment. They put ice on her foot. The ice helped her, but she was hurt for like two weeks or three weeks.

The nurse at school called my parents and told them that I might have a sprained pinky. My parents came to school as fast as possible. They took me to the emergency room. We were in the car for about fifteen minutes. When we got to the emergency room they said, "You don't have the right insurance. So go downstairs so you get to the right place."

I was worried, because what if the doctor couldn't see me? My parents were frustrated because they came all the way from work to the school, to the nurse's office, and then all the way to the emergency room, and they might not get to see a doctor.

We went into the other room, and they said, "OK. You may sit down. The doctor will be there in thirty minutes." It took the doctor an hour to arrive. He walked in and said, "What's going on? Are you hurt? Are you sick?"

I told him I hurt my pinky.

He told me to get an x-ray with a different nurse. It felt weird when they took the x-ray. I had to put my hand straight and the machine had round things that fit around my hand. They took the x-ray in about five minutes.

I went back to the room where my parents were. We had to wait about ten minutes for the x-ray to get printed and laminated. The doctor said my pinky was sprained. I was sad because now I had to miss gym and recess for a week. Gym is my place to get exercise and play sports, which I love. I felt disappointed to not be able to go to gym.

The doctor told me that the best way to treat it is to put ice on it for a week. I did that. I even had to wrap a bandana around my whole hand with ice in a bag. You know when you put ice in your mouth and you get brain freeze? It felt like that on my hand, but it was on my pinky.

In the end I could move my pinky. I even pulled it hard and twisted it. It didn't hurt. I had a full recovery.

I learned to never play in the left corner at gym, because that's where I got hurt. But if it happened again, I would know what to do. I would put ice on it for about a week. I hope it doesn't happen again so I don't have to miss gym again.

Caution: Do Not Read This Book

Joselin: The Story of a Tooth

ONCE WHEN I WAS 8 YEARS OLD, my dentist told me that if I don't pull out my tooth by April, he was going to pull it out for me. This was my first loose tooth that needed my help. My other loose teeth came out when I fell or ate something or tripped.

When I was 6, I was running down the stairs and I tripped. I rolled down the stairs. I was crying. It was so scary. All of a sudden, my two front teeth were out. They were already wiggly but they came out without my help. One tooth we found right away, the other one we never found. Never.

My mom said, "You ate it."

I asked, "How could I eat my own tooth, because it wouldn't even go down my throat?" I didn't believe her that I ate it. We looked for it for a whole week. We never found it. Nothing. I even checked the windowsill to see if the tooth was there. It wasn't.

I ate a tooth? That scared me. I thought it was disgusting. I worried it would affect everything in my body. I thought I would have to go to the hospital or the doctor so they could check me and find the tooth. But I didn't have to go to the doctor for that.

So when the dentist said he would pull out my tooth, I thought to myself, "Ahhhhhhhhh!" I was scared because if he pulled it out it would hurt so bad. My brothers had braces. When they pulled them out, there was blood. I thought it was lipstick but it was blood. When I see blood, I feel like I'm going to pass out. I thought the dentist would pull out my tooth and that there would be blood all over me. I didn't want that.

Caution: Do Not Read This Book

When I was little, I put a scary movie on T.V. There was blood all over in this movie. I wanted to pass out. It scared me. I was 4 and my mom was in the kitchen cooking. She didn't know I was watching a scary movie on accident. This is where I learned about blood.

I never wiggled my tooth because I thought it would hurt so bad. The new tooth started growing and the old tooth was on top of it. It was a big problem for me because it hurt when I ate. And when I drank milk it felt like I had a problem in my mouth. It was uncomfortable.

I got scared to take it out. My mom said, "Take it out!" but I was afraid. Then one day I wiggled it. I kept on wiggling it. And wiggling it. Then BOOM, it came out. There was a little bit of blood. I used salt water to rinse it away. All my fears about the blood coming everywhere went away.

When April came, I was so happy. The dentist checked my mouth. He said I was a brave girl. He gave me a gift for being so brave, but they didn't know how hard it was.

Caution: Do Not Read This Book

Fred: Running into Things

I ran into a trampoline.

I ran into a pot of plants.

I ran into the recycling bin by accident.

I ran into my brother. He just said, "Ouch!" because he's older.

I REMEMBER WHEN I HIT MY HEAD while looking at the Statue of Liberty. I actually did. When I was 3 I went to New York City with my mom and dad. We took a boat to see the statue. When I got there, I ran to the fence to get a better look at the statue. I was running around in circles, excited to be there. That's when I hit my head. That fence was really, really hard. My parents were surprised. They asked if I was OK. I was OK. My head hurt for like three weeks after that.

I remember when I was in Hawaii, I ran into a tree. I was with my aunt and my grandma. I was walking to the beach. I had my bathing suit on and was wearing flip-flops. Nobody pushed me. There was a vine growing along the ground. The vine was over my foot. I fell backwards when I tripped. It was a palm tree. A coconut fell out of the tree and hit the ground. I was 4 years old. The tree was soft, actually, but it hurt a little bit. It scared me, that coconut, because it came out of nowhere.

When I was 7, I ran into a wall at school. I was walking to the bathroom and then I saw my friend and said hello to him. We talked for three seconds, not a long time. When I started walking again, I didn't turn my head to see where I was going. I walked into the wall. A concrete wall. It was really hard. I hit my head on the wall. I felt dizzy and confused because I didn't see the wall. My head hurt like eight out of ten for pain. Inside my head I started yelling. That didn't help the pain. I never told anyone that I hit my head because I don't like to tell on myself.

A few days ago I ran into the door. I was in my bedroom. My sister was in my room and I was going in there to do something. She closed the door on me. I banged my head because I thought the door was open. I was outside my room holding my hand on the back of my head. I was kind of mad at her for hurting me. Where was she? She was inside my room, hiding inside my closet so that nobody could find her. She didn't want my parents to find her and get her in trouble. She got in trouble.

I ran into the birdfeeder. We had a blizzard in March of this year, 2017. We got almost two feet of snow. I had to shovel the sidewalk and the driveway. It was hard to do because there was so much snow and I couldn't pick up a lot at one time. I had to pick up a half a shovelful at one time.

Then I saw that my dad fell into the snow on the driveway. He was trying to help me shovel, but he fell because it was really windy. I helped him up. We decided to go into the house to get some hot chocolate. We were walking to the house. There was snow I didn't see. I tripped over that snow and banged my head on the birdfeeder. I felt dizzy. It hurt so bad that my mom gave me medicine that tasted like raspberries. The medicine didn't cure anything but it sure tasted good. Then we had the hot chocolate, too. My head felt the same, it still hurt, but my stomach was happy.

Nevaeh: Hissy Fits

MY LITTLE SISTER IS 2 YEARS OLD. When she doesn't get her way, she cries and throws her little fits.

It all started when she was one. My mom was taking a video of her lying down with her feet in the air. My mom was joking and told her to sit up. My sister slowly moved her head back and forth in a "no" motion, and my mom said that was the first time she ever said, "No" to us.

I was giggling in the video because I thought that it was funny that she was saying no to my mom. That's when we knew that she was going to say "No" to us and not listen.

Now that she's 2, she knows how to walk and talk and grab and scream and kick.

When my sister sees the cat, she'll go over to it and say, "Kitty!" and then she'll grab the tail. The cat will turn around and hiss at her. My sister will let go, but then she'll do it again or touch its paws or nose. How does she know which spots will bother my cat the most? My cat doesn't like her. If he were a person, every time she walked in the room he would tell her, "Get away from me!"

This morning she got my mom's Jolly Rancher bag and poured it on the floor. My mom said that she could not have one. She started to kick and scream. My mom sneezed, and my sister stopped crying and said in a regular voice, "God bless you."

My mom said thank you and told her that she still was not getting a Jolly Rancher. My sister begged and said "Please" in a high voice and stretched the word out for a long time. She didn't get what she wanted. She screamed, waved her hands up and down and kicked her legs. Mom gave her a look and told her to stop it, and she sort of stopped it, she sat there moaning.

She steps on my legs when she doesn't get her way. She cries, screams and she even bites. She bit me because I only gave her one piece of my mom's candy. She wanted more. I said no. So she bit me. Later when she had a snack and I asked for some, she said, "OK," and then put it in her mouth and ate it right in front of me. I'm not really angry at her because she's a baby, but that's not fair.

Next time I have something she's not getting any, which really means I will still give it to her because she's a baby. It is the kind of thing that bugs me at that moment and then after a while I get over it.

Sometimes my mom and my aunt and I are sitting relaxing, and my sister sneaks upstairs to see Grandpa. We don't even know she's there until we hear this loud BOOM BOOM BOOM, which is her running across his room. Then my mom will say, "Go get your sister." Usually I'll say "OK," but I'll just sit there and keep on playing so my mom has to remind me again. It's annoying that I have to stop what I'm doing to go and get her all the time.

If I'm playing with a toy and she wants to play with it, she'll just grab it out of my hand and say, "Mine!" Sometimes I give it to her and sometimes I don't give it to her. It depends on what mood I'm in. If I came home from school and I was doing my homework, and she made me angry and upset I would say, "No. It's my homework. I have to do it." And if she says, "It's mine!" my mom or my aunt will tell her to leave me alone because I'm doing my homework.

If I was drawing something and she said, "Sissy, can I draw, too?" I would give her that drawing and let her do it, and I would get another piece of paper for myself.

If I'm sitting down and just chilling, like watching T.V. or playing on my phone, and she kicks me and grabs me, I'll just scream at her and say, "You're annoying me. Leave me alone!"

But when she's just sitting and playing with her ducky that floats and has a purple jacket, or when she's sitting in her chair watching T.V., I don't have to worry about her as much. I know she's quiet and entertained and she'll leave me alone.

Sometimes she'll say, "I wov you!" and she'll give me a kiss that leaves drool on my face. I'll wipe off my face and kiss her back, because she's a baby and she didn't just spit on me on purpose.

I do love her more than all the words in the world, but if she's being annoying I have to remind myself that she's just a baby and she doesn't know better.

Luckily, I know better.

Caution: Do Not Read This Book

Caution: Do Not Read This Book

Jorge: About Soccer

I LOVE SOCCER. My whole family are soccer fans. We like the team Barcelona. They live and practice their soccer in a stadium in Spain. The stadium's name is Camp Nou. They are the best team because they have all the good players.

One of their players is our favorite. His name is Messi. He's the best soccer player in the whole world. He can do tricks like dribbling the ball with his foot. He can pass the ball past four or five players, which is hard to do because there are a lot of players going for that ball. He kicks the ball just right to make the goal. In his career he made like 135 goals.

Caution: Do Not Read This Book

He is a shy person. I know that because my dad told me. I like shy people because I can make friends with them. When they go to lunch they sit by themselves and I can sit with them. If Messi were in my school, he would sit with older kids because he's famous. But I'd still like him.

I like that he laughs a lot. His friends make a lot of jokes and he laughs. I like to laugh, too. We are the same because we both like to laugh. We are also the same because I have a shirt with his name on the back. I'm close to his number. I'm number 9 when I play soccer and he's number 10. His son and I kind of look the same.

Soccer season already started. I don't know what days they play. My dad just calls me downstairs to watch. They played last night against PSG. I was almost about to cry because Barcelona had to make six goals to win. There were only 36 seconds left and they made a goal. They won. A lot of people thought they weren't going to make it, but they did. Everybody on T.V. was crying and screaming with happiness.

Caution: Do Not Read This Book

My dad said that Barcelona is still going for winning, PSG is out now. I was happy because they won. I don't know when they play again, but I'll be watching.

Caution: Do Not Read This Book

Caution: Do Not Read This Book

Aurora: Oaxaca, Mexico

ONE SUMMER MY MOM sent me to Oaxaca, Mexico for vacation. I went to meet relatives from my mom and dad's families. I stayed with my aunt sometimes, and sometimes I stayed with my grandmother or my other grandmother.

I did a lot of things when I was there. One day we woke up early to travel to a public pool so we could spend the day swimming. My mom's mom made Mexican pizza, which was good. It had avocado, lettuce, cheese and beans on it.

There were these chocolate eggs that had presents inside. I got a doll that I had to build. My cousin took me on a motorcycle ride. It was like a bicycle, but a lot faster. And noisier. I helped my grandmother make tortillas. We went to the store and bought dough and put it in a press that squishes it together. It came out like a tortilla that you buy at the store, but it wasn't cooked yet. Sometimes when we cooked them, we got a bubble from when air got inside the tortilla. The bubble would go back down when you touched it.

I got to drink an oatmeal drink with hot chocolate. It was like hot chocolate, but in the end you have to eat the oatmeal that tastes like chocolate, too. I played in water that had crabs. I was afraid of those crabs because the claws could pinch me.

We did so many things, but there are two things I remember the most. We went to a fair and we went on a zip line.

My aunt took my cousins and me to the fair. It was a fair like we have here, but it was different. There were no seatbelts on the rides! The rides were expensive, so I got to go on only two. I went on the bumper cars and the dragon that went from side to side.

My aunt bought me a pet. The pet was a lizard. She had these pointy things on the back of her head. She was green and about as long as a hand and a half. She was pretty quiet and calm. We kept her in a cage at my aunt's house. I named her Pearl.

I kept Pearl in the same cage as my sister's lizard. Hers was a boy. I wasn't watching when the terrible thing happened. The boy lizard killed my Pearl. I was really sad. Then late at night when I was sleeping, my aunt fed Pearl to the dogs. She just threw her out to the dogs and the three dogs fought over her. Luckily she did it when I was sleeping so I didn't have to watch.

My grandma took me to a park that had a zip line. Grandma let me go on the zip line. It was one of the most amazing things I ever got to go on. It was like you were going down really quick, like you were falling down a building. I thought I would crash into a tree at the end of the ride. I thought I would fall off the zip line and onto the ground.

My cousin went first because he was ready first. I watched him go. I thought he was going to yell and be afraid, but he didn't. He went on the zip line many times before.

I got hooked up for my turn. It felt like I was hanging from a tree. They hooked me up with a really thick rope so if I fell down I would just be hanging. The thing that held me up was around my legs so it didn't choke me. The other activities at the park felt safer. This felt scary.

To get started they had to push me to get me going. I thought I was going to fall to my death. I didn't. I started screaming. I had to pick up my feet and grab onto the rope. It felt like someone was picking me up from my legs. That first ride was too scary to have a good time. At the end I felt like really excited to be there. Right at the end I knew I wanted to do it again. I did.

It wasn't a free ride. We had to pay every time we went down. I loved the zip line. My cousins and my little sister loved it too. We went on it like five times. At first we yelled when we went down, but then we got used to it and laughed during the ride.

Once I left Oaxaca, my aunt was really sad. She didn't want to let me go. I felt the same. It was so exciting there that I didn't want to leave. Maybe when I'm grown up and with my own children, then I can go back so my kids can see how great Mexico is.

Caution: Do Not Read This Book

Manny: I Love the Snow

Outside when it snows, it feels like I'm in a snow heaven. It looks like clouds are white and there's white everywhere. The snow on the ground feels like I am walking on a big, fluffy cloud. My heart is pumping slower because it's cold out. I like the snow.

I like to play in the snow. I don't just want to look at the snow because it will hurt my eyes. I want to be in the snow. We have snowball fights. My brother and sister throw most of the snowballs at me, but I mostly dodge them.

It's fun to play in the snow because when my mom and grandma are inside, they look outside and they laugh at how silly we are. I am always on my hands and knees and scooting side to side. Sometimes my brother throws a snowball too hard and it gives my sister and me a bruise, but we're OK after about two minutes.

Once it snowed super hard. There was a slide of snow and every time it snowed, it rebuilt the slide. My neighbors and I always were sliding down it in the winter. It was fun because when it rebuilt, it made like a staircase. It was like a toy slide made out of snow. We played on it about five times, and then we just looked at it and remembered how much fun it was to slide down.

Once I walked up the slide. I was scared that everyone would be mad at me because I kind of ruined the slide. But then when it snowed, my footprints were covered up. They went away. It was kind of like a crime scene with my footprints all over the slide, and then the snow filled them in.

I thought I would play on the slide for a lot of winters and remember how fun it was when I was little, but then my neighbors dug up the slide because there were flowers there. I kind of get why they dug up the slide. They wanted their flowers out and they didn't want their money from planting them to go to waste.

There are many more things about the snow that I love. The next time it snows, I am going to plop in it and I will laugh for at least ten seconds.

Caution: Do Not Read This Book

Caution: Do Not Read This Book

KATHERINE: SCARED AT THE MALL

I WENT SHOPPING WITH MY MOM and my baby brother. I wanted to go to the toy store. My mom said I could go there, but first I had to take care of my baby brother while she shopped for clothes at Burlington. I was OK with that.

My job was hard. I had to watch him. He just wanted to crawl out of his little Mickey Mouse car. I gave him a lollypop that I had in my purse. The candy kept him from crying and screaming because he wanted to run around and take all the clothes off the racks.

It was a hard job.

Then we went to the mall.

My mom said I could go to the toy store, but I had to stay there. I couldn't walk around. She said, "You gotta stay in the toy store."

I said, "OK." I thought I would stay there.

She left me and I started shopping. I wanted to buy a Barbie. But then I looked at another toy and I liked it more. It was a puppy that could bark and walk. I had ten dollars to spend at the toy store. It cost $8.99. I had enough money to buy the puppy. I paid for it and left the store.

My mom made me promise to stay in the store. But I left.

I walked around the mall. I watched the other kids walking around. I went to Mom's favorite store, Charlotte Russe, to see if she was in there. She wasn't there. I went to the shoe store, Payless. She wasn't there, either. I kept looking for her.

I was thinking about my mom and how she said that I couldn't leave the toy store. I felt bad and mad at myself for not listening to my mom. I went back to the toy store. My mom wasn't there.

I was worried that she left and went home without me. Usually my stepdad tells my mom that if I don't stay in the correct store, they might leave me there. I was feeling upset and worried. Where did my mom go?

Then I remembered that my brother liked to go to Fun-E-Farm. It's where you have a lot of bouncy houses and you jump all around. They have one in the mall.

It wasn't hard to find. I walked there. I couldn't go in because I didn't have one of those bracelets that show I've paid. I looked in the window and saw my mom sitting at a table. I called her name and she saw me.

I said, "I finally found you!"

She wasn't mad at me for finding her. I showed her my new toy. She said next time she will go with me to the toy store. She bought me a wristband so I could go into Fun-E-Farm. I felt happy to be with my mom again.

Caution: Do Not Read This Book

Carlos: Visiting My Cousins

EARLY ONE MORNING, my dad woke me up. He has black hair and brown eyes. He said that we were going to New York City to visit my cousins. I was so happy. I hadn't seen my cousins for three years and three months. I missed them so much.

The last time I saw my cousins, we played at their house in the city. We played hide and seek because they have a huge, huge house. They have a gaming room. There's this little hole in the ceiling. I climbed up there and climbed into the vent and I crawled through the vent.

It's clean in there. It has a bar with plugs. It's so nice up there I thought I could bring a little T.V. up there, and plug it in and just watch cartoons or something. I've been in the vent before. Last time I crawled through the vent and ended up in the kitchen. I got a snack and then went back in the vent. In the end I got bored waiting for them to find me so I climbed out.

My dad and I went on the bus for our visit. My mom couldn't go because she was sick and my brothers were at daycare. The bus ride was horrible. It was so bumpy. I got bored sitting there and going there. I didn't want to go to the restroom on the bus and I had to go. I had to hold it all the way to my cousin's house. I sat on the bus and edited my YouTube channel on my I-Pad.

When we got to my cousin's house, my dad was happy. He gave a hug to my uncle and he said, "Nice to see you again!" My dad and his brother sat down to play cards. I couldn't believe that they sat and played cards for five hours and didn't use the restroom.

When we got there, I was embarrassed. I forgot my one cousin's name. I only remembered two of them. The other one I didn't remember at all because he was a little tiny baby.

I played with my cousins for an hour. We played hide and seek again, but I didn't go to the vent. Then we played in my cousin's gaming room because he has the most games. He has the little machines. We spent our time together. We got snacks and watched the movie *Transformers 5*, and then we watched the first Transformer movie. We got out their art stuff, like panda stuff that we stuck on a plate. We also colored superhero stuff. I colored Goku and my cousins colored different ones.

When it was time to go, I locked myself in the gaming room because I didn't want to go. My cousin gave my dad the key. He was opening the door when my mom called. She said we could stay for a sleepover. My dad said, "OK." We stayed at their house overnight. We watched another movie and stayed up late.

I can't wait to go back for another visit. I hope I have a lot of fun there again.

Caution: Do Not Read This Book

MASSIEL: I LOVE CHOCOLATE

I LOVE CHOCOLATE. I usually get it on church days. Mom lets us go to the mall and get a treat. I usually choose chocolate candies or chocolate ice cream. I really love dark chocolate with cocoa. I usually like chocolate even though it's not good for my body. I just eat a little bit at a time.

I usually sneak my mom's chocolate. She likes to hide it in her room or in the refrigerator. She doesn't know I ate it. She thinks she already ate it, or she tries to find it. Sometimes I tell my brother, "Go and get Mommy's chocolate for me." He does. Then he gets in trouble. I know this is a little tricky, but I love chocolate so much.

When my mom goes to the bathroom, my dad sneaks her chocolate, too. She says to my brother, "Did you eat my chocolate?" And he says, "That was Dad, not me." She says she will have to eat Dad's torta later to get him back. She's lucky because my brother doesn't sneak her treats. He likes to sneak cereal.

Yesterday I tried to sneak into Mom's room when she was sleeping so I could get the chocolate on her desk. But even though she was sleeping, she heard me. She said, "Go watch T.V. I'm sick. Let me sleep."

On my birthday, my uncles bring me a box of chocolate or a chocolate cake. I like to eat the chocolate right at my party. Sometimes my little cousin, who is 3 years old, asks for just one piece of my birthday candy. I tell her, "No. They're mine." Then she'll go to my mom and complain that I won't share, and my mom will give her a piece of her chocolate, which is good because I get to eat my own.

Caution: Do Not Read This Book

I like every kind of chocolate, but I just don't like it with peanut butter. I don't like peanut butter, even though I haven't tasted it. Some people in my family are allergic to it, so we don't have it in my house.

When it was Valentine's Day, I got chocolates. I got one box from my mom and another one from my teacher. I also got a Valentine's balloon. My dad gave me a stuffed animal with chocolate. I ate most of my chocolate that day. At the end of the day I only had two more candies left. I felt sad because my brother had more than I had.

I think I will get tired of eating candy one day. Maybe I'll get sick of eating too much sugar. When I have children, I will share my treats with my children. If they sneak my candies from me, I won't get mad. I'll remember that I used to do that to my mom, too.

Caution: Do Not Read This Book

Caution: Do Not Read This Book

Victor: The Wrong Store

Normally my days are fun. I go outside and play football with my friends. I might go to a birthday party and eat ice cream. I might play video games with my brother and try to beat him. Sometimes I like to ride my bike around the block.

One day my mom said we could go to New Jersey to visit my dad's cousins. On the way she said we could go shopping. I like to go shopping because I don't have to be at home just being bored. I like to get new shoes, new shirts and video games.

I felt excited about going on the trip. I had never met Dad's cousins and I got to go shopping in some different stores. We were going to go just for the day. We put on clean clothes and stopped at a gas station to get some snacks for the trip. It was going to be a three-hour drive. That wasn't a very long trip for me because on another trip, I went to Virginia and that was a lot longer in the car.

There were four of us in the car. My mom and dad were sitting in the front, my brother and I were in the back. I was bored during the car ride. I tried to sleep. I couldn't. I traded Pokémon cards with my brother, which we love to do. I took a little nap, like thirty minutes. When my dad woke me up he said, "We're at the stores." So I woke up right away.

I wanted to buy a car with a controller. My dad said I could get it if I behaved at school and at home, but that he would take it away if I didn't behave at school or at home. I wanted the car for a long time. This is the day I was going to get it.

The four people in my family walked into the store. I thought I would go to the boy's section. But when

I walked through the doors, I was surprised. All I could see was pink and purple things. All I could see was girls' stuff. It was a new store I had never heard of and I didn't see anything there for boys.

My brother said, "Oh my gosh. This is going to be the boringest thing on earth!"

I said, "Yeah, that's true."

My mom wanted new clothes and new high heels for a party. She wanted me to pick which pair of shoes was better. I told her both, because I didn't want to be there. She said we would only be there for five minutes. I was not sad about staying there a short time. But after five minutes, the time we would be there got longer and longer.

My dad said he didn't want to be there, either, because he wanted to buy a new shirt. He told my mom to stay there and that he could take us to another place. Mom said, "OK," because then she would have more time getting her new stuff.

We left my mom in the store and my dad took us to other places to buy things. We got a snack in a place that had milkshakes, some new clothes that we got to try on first, and that remote control car I wanted.

As soon as I got my new car I was excited because I really wanted it. I wanted to play with it. I didn't want to shop any more because I wanted to play with my new car. My dad wanted us to go back to the store where my mother was.

I thought that we had to stay in that store a long time again. But we didn't have to. When we got there Mom went to pay.

I want to go shopping again, but not in a store that only sells stuff for girls.

Heavenlee: Gymnastics

I STARTED GYMNASTICS when I was 4 years old. I knew how to do a split when I was 4. Then I stopped for a while and started doing gymnastics again when I was 7. We had a competition when I was 7. I went on the balance beam, did a floor routine and had an event on the uneven bars.

The balance beam was hard. I had to do a back tuck, which is when you stand up, put your hands up, then you go down and flip. I did it right. Then I had to do a split; I had to put my legs out until I'm flat on the beam. Next I had to do a cartwheel on the beam. It's easy. You stand

Caution: Do Not Read This Book

with your hands up, then you put one leg up and flip in the air. You have to land on your feet. I nailed the routine.

For the floor routine I had to dance to the song "Thunderbolt." This was a confusing routine because the music goes slow and then fast and then slow. First I ran and jumped and did a split in the air and landed on my feet. You have to run in slow motion and then you run fast to the end of the mat. Next you have to do a back flip, jump, fall, split in the air and then land on your feet.

The uneven bar routine was hard. I had to go to the low bar and swing to the high bar. Then on the high bar, I had to turn on it and jump off and land on the low one again. It was a tough routine because I had to go from the low bar to the high bar and back to the low bar. It's hard to do that because you have to figure out, like a math equation, what the space equals. You have to really focus. If you don't focus, you can fall and injure your knee or your ankle.

I still do gymnastics today. Every Thursday I go to the Little Gym to practice. My coaches are Brianna,

Brittney, and Mr. C. I like gymnastics. My grandma did it first, then my mom took after her mother. Now I'm taking after my mother. So this is the third generation of women in my family who love gymnastics.

I don't care about winning awards. I only care about focusing, practicing, following directions and doing my best. I love gymnastics!

Caution: Do Not Read This Book

Caution: Do Not Read This Book

Lisbeth: Sea Adventure

THERE ARE MANY THINGS I wanted for my birthday when I turned 7. I wanted nail polish, more LEGOs, and some of those dolls called Shopkins. I got the nail polish. I didn't get the LEGOs and I only got one Shopkins. My last gift was a surprise.

My dad said to me, "Do you want to go to the sea?"

I had never been to the sea before. I had always wanted to go. I was worried about sharks eating me, or maybe they would eat my family and I would be alone.

My uncle kept telling me about the mermaids in the ocean and how they looked nice. I thought there really were mermaids. I wanted to see them and go with them on top of the water and talk with them.

My uncle told me about this mermaid called "Aqua Marine." He showed me the movie with two girls who find her in a pool at the sea. I remember that her nails kept changing colors and she talked a lot with the dolphins.

I wanted to play with Aqua Marine and her dolphins.

I said, "Yes, Daddy. I want to go to the sea. And also can we see Aqua Marine?"

He said, "Who's that?"

I tried to explain but he told me that mermaids don't exist.

I thought he was wrong.

We invited all my aunts and uncles to come with us. Some did not come because it was too far, or they had an appointment at the dentist or the doctor. Some didn't have the money to spend on a short trip.

Caution: Do Not Read This Book

When we were driving there, I slept a lot. My mom gave me her phone to play on because I was bored sitting there in the car.

When I first saw the sea I was shocked. There was a bunch of water! I'd never seen that much water before. I made my dad unlock the door to get out of the car, and I brought a mermaid doll with me that my aunt gave me for Christmas. I took it with me because I thought I would see Aqua Marine and I would show her my doll.

We got out of the car and I kept yelling, "Aqua Marine. Aqua Marine. Where are you?"

My dad finally said, "Aqua Marine is not here."

I was sad because I wanted to see her.

Everyone arrived. We got the table out. We made hot dogs and hamburgers on a grill that was already there. We had our picnic on the parking lot.

I was looking at the beach. I tried to run to it, but my cousins showed me their Shopkins to distract me from running off. It worked a little bit. I looked back and ran to my uncle who just arrived. I hugged him and forgot about the beach for a few minutes.

My mom took me to the bathroom on the beach and took off my clothes. My bathing suit was under them. She brought those things that you can float on, and she tied one to a little stick she found and stuck the stick in the sand.

All my cousins came and we kept on playing in the water. The water was kind of clean and kind of dirty. I found a fish in the water that they said was a clown fish. I knew how to swim a little bit. I kicked the water. I splashed around with my cousins.

One time I sank in the water and the water went up my nose. I started coughing because the water got up in my nose. My mom got a tissue and helped me clean the water out. Then I went right back in. The water was cold. I took my mermaid doll into the water and I almost lost her. She got out of my hands and was floating away. I yelled to my cousin and he got the doll. I hugged her and put her on the table where we were having lunch so she wouldn't float away again.

I will always remember that it was fun to go with my whole family to the beach and that my little doll mermaid came with me. Maybe we will go to the beach again this summer. If we go, I don't think I'll bring that doll. I'd rather bring my journal to write in.

Caution: Do Not Read This Book

Toby: LEGOs

LEGOS ARE FUN. If I got a brand new box of LEGOs, I'd open the box, then I'd open the bags that are inside of it. Then I'd pour out the LEGOs, but I wouldn't sort them. It's a little more fun to just look for the LEGOs, to dig through them. If you sort them, then everything would be with other pieces that are the same color, and it would be harder to find them, because they'd blend in.

Then I'd open up the instructions and I'd start building with what it says. It can be kind of hard, because the instructions don't have any words. They just show you pictures. Sometimes the pictures are more like diagrams. I look at the picture of the LEGO piece I need, and I try to find it. Then I look at the picture of what that step should look like after I put the LEGOs together. Then I put them on the actual structure to do that step.

Sometimes it doesn't go exactly right and I have to redo it. Sometimes I haven't done exactly what the directions showed because it's hard to tell what the directions are showing. I redo it if it's not correct. It can be frustrating if you get a step wrong, but then it's really fun once you get it right.

When I do it the right way, that feels good. If you get the directions correct, then you just move on to the next step. It keeps on going like that.

As you keep working on the kit, it gets bigger and bigger. At first it looks like a couple of tiny pieces, and then it starts to look like what it's supposed to look like. It looks better as it grows. When I built a tree house, I started to be able to put more parts on it that moved in interesting ways. But not all LEGOs can move, and that's okay.

Caution: Do Not Read This Book

Each step that you take when you're building a LEGO set gets more exciting, because each step gets you closer to being able to play with it. And when I finish it, I feel really great about it. I feel proud that I followed the directions and made something that looks good.

A LEGO dragon that I built, after I finished, I took it apart so I could build the same thing again. I left some of the pieces together, like the head, and some pieces I had to put together from scratch, and I put all the parts back together. Some LEGO kits, after you build them, you just play with them.

If there's anything that moves in a finished LEGO set, you can move that around. If there are humans involved, you can play with the humans by moving them around and having them do different things.

We also have a box of LEGOs that are all different kinds of pieces that can let you build a lot of different kinds of things. It used to have directions for how to build a fire truck, a house with a dog inside of it, and a few other things, but I ripped up those directions one time when I was really frustrated. So now when you use that box of LEGOs, you do things that you want to do, and you can't use instructions, which also turns out to be kind of fun. I've ended up making things like a giant box thing on wheels, a swimming pool, and a couple of different kinds of cars.

I like doing both kinds of LEGOs, but I prefer the ones with instructions. Then you get to play with things that have a lot of cool stuff and that actually look like real things.

I hope you enjoyed my story about LEGOs. (If you'd like to learn more about LEGOs, go to Wikipedia. On the LEGO website, you can see many different kits that they make and you can do games and stuff.

Caution: Do Not Read This Book

Opal: What I Imagine When I'm Bored

SOMETIMES WHEN I'M BORED, I don't feel like playing with dolls or petting my rabbits. I usually like to talk, but when I'm bored I don't want to talk a lot. I get this way when I run out of ideas. Usually I have a lot of ideas. Sometimes I get bored when things don't go my way, because I had something on my mind and when it didn't work, I didn't have another idea.

I'm always thinking but it's not as easy to think when I'm bored. It takes a long time to get in a thinking mood. Sometimes I wonder what it would be like if I weren't me. What if I were a doll? I would be a happy and

Caution: Do Not Read This Book

smart doll with very strong feelings. I would look like I look now. What if I were a doll and there were children playing with me?

The children would like me, but sometimes they would get mad about things and think it was my fault. I wouldn't be able to talk to them, but I would be able to talk to the other dolls about it. Because when I imagine this, I imagine the whole world as a dollhouse.

One person would have all the dollhouses with one big house for every continent. And that person would decide to split the people up to different places. Each place would be different. The person would decide where you would fit the most, like for your personality.

What would it be like if children were playing with me? It would usually be fun, but maybe I wouldn't like the way the child was playing with me, or how they were making the world go. I wouldn't be able to communicate with the child to suggest changes.

I'm glad in this life I have my own choices, like what I want to eat or how my day goes and how I act. I get to decide what I want to wear every day. If I were a doll, other people would choose what I eat and what I wear.

I like being able to speak out. I can talk about my feelings and how I feel things are going and how they might change. If I want to change something that I don't feel is going right, I can talk about it. Being able to communicate is important to me. I can still communicate with my friend, Allison, who moved to Germany, by talking on the phone or writing her letters. I like being able to talk and tell people what I want to say.

And I can tell people how I feel, not just my friends. I'm glad that I have more ways to communicate with other people than I would if I were in the dollhouse. If I were in a dollhouse, I would be separate from the other dolls in different places. I'm glad I'm able to communicate with other people, for real.

The best part of being alive is having a family to talk to about things bothering me that I don't feel comfortable telling others about, and knowing they can help me fix these problems.

I wonder about what it would be like to be a doll, but I'm glad I'm a human, alive!

Caution: Do Not Read This Book

KENYA: JAMAICA

I ONLY WENT TO JAMAICA ONCE. My aunt lives there and other family members. My mom and I went when I was younger, like 4 years old. We took an airplane.

The airplane ride there wasn't fun. There were these people on the plane who were flying for the first time. They all threw up, all ten of them. It's really true. The whole plane smelled like poop.

My mom said, "We need to get off this plane, now!" She doesn't like the smell of puke.

I thought I would puke, but I didn't. I was gagging. Now when I think of flying on a plane, I think about that smell and I don't want to fly again.

We landed in Jamaica. It was a relief to get there. The air of Jamaica smelled like food. Like lots of food. It smelled like chicken and pork because there were people grilling food on the sidewalk that was for sale. I wanted to buy some of that food, and we did. We bought a pineapple colada (without alcohol) and some Jerk Chicken. It was really good.

We went to our hotel. There was a pool with a big glass window that looked out at the ocean. It was a magnificent piece of glass, so cool! There was lots of food at the hotel. There was chicken and there was rice, and mangos and more mangos. There was a lot of fruit because we were close to where the fruit grows. It's really hot there so the fruit grows really well.

It was time to go to my uncle's house. He lives in like a huge mansion. We didn't stay there because we had a hotel room. It was the first time I ever met him. He was really old, like maybe 56 years old. He is my mom's brother. We hugged him hello and then went to the beach.

The beach was nearby. He had a beach house. It was really cool. The sand at the beach was a pink color. I didn't know sand could be pink, because we didn't have any pink sand in the United States. I had my bathing suit on. We went into the water. The ocean was saltwater but it was so clean that it looked more like pool water. The waves were really high because there was about to be a storm. They crashed on the beach.

I made a sandcastle in the sand. It came out taller than I was because my mom helped me make it. It was fun to make because I had never built a sandcastle before. Never. I was the boss and I told my mom what to do, then she was the boss and told me what to do. The castle came out fantastic.

I went on a surfboard with my friend. It was my first time on a board. It was really tricky. The board was hard to balance because it was sitting on the water and it kept sinking down. I sat on the board for a while. When I got used to it, I tried to stand up. That was a little tricky because the board was moving a lot. I told that board to stay still. It wouldn't.

I was able to stand up when there was a wave. It was a little scary. Would I lose control? What if I can't find my mom? I was very worried and had trouble focusing. Where was my mom? She was on the beach. Would I be able to find her? In the end I did stand up on that board, but only for a moment. Then I fell in the water.

What I liked about Jamaica was how beautiful it was. There was a whole bunch of coconut trees. I had never seen one before. I learned about Jamaica before I went there, but being there was different than looking at a picture. It was more beautiful than looking at a picture. There was a forest in the background. The palm trees went all the way up.

There were monkeys on the trees. I saw some in cages. They told me that they put all of the girls in one cage and all of the boys in another cage so they wouldn't play together. The monkeys were dirty, but they were cute with their cheeks popping out. They wanted to meet people so they could get more attention.

They use different words in Jamaica. Almost everyone could speak so I could understand them. I learned how to say, "Hey mon!" And they laugh a lot, even when they're speaking. They wore tight t-shirts and shorts and sandals. A lot of people played drums.

I'll always remember the wind. The wind was blowing food away and blowing papers. There was always a good breeze, which helped so the sun didn't feel too hot. Before the storm there was a nice breeze and a little rain. During the storm there was a tornado, so we had to go inside a place that had a basement without windows. I could hear the wind blowing when we were down there. It was exciting but a little scary, too. There was a lot of damage from the wind when we came back out. One house was on fire because someone left the stove on. It looked like there was an earthquake because some of the ground looked like it came up and out.

Caution: Do Not Read This Book

If someone else wants to go to Jamaica, I would tell that person to go. But watch out for the storms. Go on a day when they're not going to have a storm. And you should try the pineapple colada and the Jerk Chicken.

Caution: Do Not Read This Book

Caution: Do Not Read This Book

Caution: Do Not Read This Book

Acknowledgements:

We would like to thank many people.

We want to thank our parents for driving us to school early in the morning. We thank ourselves for waking up early in the morning. We thank Miss Sharon and Miss Holly for teaching us. We thank Miss Val for encouraging us to publish and sell books. We thank KALP for funding our publishing class. We thank Miss Erin for helping make this KALP program happen and letting us use her classroom. We are thanking the PTO for helping us sell the books.

Caution: Do Not Read This Book

Caution: Do Not Read This Book

Biographies

Caution: Do Not Read This Book

Caution: Do Not Read This Book

Aurora

I LIKE ICE CREAM IN THE WINTER. I got a fish for Christmas. My birthday is in the spring, sometimes on Easter Sunday. I like Tres Leches cake. I'm a middle child. I enjoy chocolate dip. Steak is my favorite food. I love playing in the snow. I dedicate my story to my family.

Carlos

I'M CARLOS. My favorite thing to do is do tricks on my bike. The best thing I ever ate was chocolate cake that sat in a puddle of more chocolate. My friends and I like to go on Pokémon hunts. I would like to dedicate my story to my whole family.

Caution: Do Not Read This Book

Fred

I LIKE PIZZA WITH EXTRA CHEESE. I like lions, but don't talk about alligators. I like sneaking up on people and scaring them. My cat is gray and white. She likes scratching people and tickling their feet. I dedicate this to my cat, because she never ran into me.

Caution: Do Not Read This Book

Heavenlee

I'M A FOURTH-GRADER NAMED HEAVENLEE. I like to dance, especially hip-hop. My favorite color is blue because it's bright, shiny, and the color of the sky. I have a lot of cousins. When I'm outside of school, my favorite things to do are going for walks, playing with my puppy, and climbing trees. I would like to dedicate this to my best cousin, Nevaeh, because she is cheerful, a great artist, and she inspires me.

Caution: Do Not Read This Book

Johnny

I'M A NINE-YEAR-OLD FORTH-GRADER. I have been playing soccer since I was 3 years old. I really like to play soccer. I like to listen to music on snow days. I also like to hang out with my friends. Furthermore, I like to have snowball fights with my parents or just spend time with my parents. I don't like spiders or snakes because they are venomous. I also don't like falling from heights. Lastly I don't like tomatoes, pickles or olives. I'd like to dedicate this to my parents because they have taught me so many things.

Caution: Do Not Read This Book

Jorge

I WOULD LIKE TO DEDICATE THIS to the best soccer player in the world, Lionel Messi. I'll do anything for Messi. Soccer is my life. It's the best sport. I like Barcelona so much.

Caution: Do Not Read This Book

Joselin

I AM AN ALMOST TEN-YEAR-OLD who loves pink. I love math because you don't have to do storytelling. I love talking. Some people even call me a chatterbox. I like fashion and experiment with designing dresses. I would like to dedicate this book to Miss Holly and Miss Sharon.

Katherine

HI. MY NAME IS KATHERINE. I am 9 years old. I am in fourth grade. My favorite colors are hot pink, blue and purple. Playing soccer makes me happy. My favorite food is pasta. I dedicate my story to my family.

Kenya

I AM KENYA AND I AM A FUNNY GIRL. I am 9 years old and I want to be a doctor when I grow up. My favorite colors are teal, neon yellow and neon pink. My favorite food is ice cream. My favorite thing to do is gymnastics. I wish I could eat peanut butter brownies...but I'm allergic to them. Darn it! I dedicate this book to the people who raised me.

Lisbeth

I LOVE RABBITS BUT NOT SPIDERS. I like to play my viola. I have a sister named Katherine. I like playing soccer, but I don't like playing volleyball. I like organizing my papers, but don't ask me about organizing my bedroom. I dedicate my story to my family.

Caution: Do Not Read This Book

Manny

I DON'T LIKE SPIDERS. I like snakes, but not for food. Bears are cool, but not as a gigantic pet. I love the snow but not the slippery ice. I love my family, but not when they fight. I like cellos and drums. I dedicate my story to Miss Holly and Miss Sharon because they helped me with everything in the book.

Caution: Do Not Read This Book

Massiel

HI. MY NAME IS MASSIEL. I like to be with friends. Sometimes we get into a little trouble. I also like pizza. I am 9 years old. My favorite color is pink. I am in fourth grade. I dedicate this to my cousin Shallymar.

Caution: Do Not Read This Book

Nevaeh

MY NAME IS NEVAEH and I dedicate this to my cousin, Suzy. She is the only one that I'm excited to see. I love to play tag with my friends. Outside on the playground I love to talk about how boring math is with my friends. I dedicate this to my best friends for always being on my side.

Caution: Do Not Read This Book

Opal

I LOVE TO PLAY WITH MY BUNNIES. I like to dress fancy. I love to sing while looking at myself in the mirror.

My favorite book series in the world is Harry Potter. I hate avocados, they make me feel like I'm going to puke. Me and my older sister get into arguments, but we have gotten better about compromising. I get upset when there are not any snow days.

Caution: Do Not Read This Book

I love to write fiction and nonfiction. I really like gymnastics because it makes me strong and it's fun. I dedicate this book to my family. They have helped me write and they encourage me.

Caution: Do Not Read This Book

Piper

YOU DON'T KNOW ME, but I love to draw. I also love to go camping. I do not like spiders. I love to go hiking. I like to go to the fair but don't like the rollercoasters. I do not like the heat, but I love the cold. I dedicate this book to my dad because he taught me how to draw, and to my family for being there for me all the time. I also want to thank my friends because if they weren't in my life, then life would not be the same.

Caution: Do Not Read This Book

Toby

IF YOU PROMISE TO GIVE ME $1,000, I will write this. I love to sleep and am a math whiz! Reading is my passion. I love watching T.V. I hate snow days and I really hate cleaning the toilet. Do not make me clean the cat! I really hate cleaning cats and dogs. I'd like to dedicate this book to my family.

Caution: Do Not Read This Book

Victor

I AM AN OUTSIDE KID. I like to play outside because it is awesome. I like to play sports. My favorite sports are football, soccer and basketball. I love to go to water parks. I like all of the water parks in the United States. I dedicate my story to my family.

Caution: Do Not Read This Book

Caution: Do Not Read This Book

Afterward: The Game of Writing

KENYA, A GIRL IN THE PUBLISHING CLASS, studied the words on my computer screen. "It would be better if we added, 'and have more grit' to the second paragraph."

"Good one," I said as I added her words and read them out loud.

"Please read slower," Opal said, concentrating on the words.

I slowed the pace of my reading, ecstatic that they were taking their writing assignment seriously.

These two third-graders were chosen to write the introduction to this book. Today they were editing their ideas.

"Can you read it again?" Kenya asked.

I read slowly.

"Wait." Opal tapped my computer screen. "I just learned about this in my class." She pointed to one word. "You can't start a sentence with the word, 'but.'"

I smiled. Though Sharon and I hadn't forced grammar rules on this group of seventeen students who showed up early mornings to write, I had banned words from former kid-writers. Once I put some middle school students on a "really" diet where they could only write that word once a month. I temporarily forbade another group of students from ever writing the word "because," because I was tired of building independent clauses.

So began a mini lesson on how to use conjunctions as sentence starters. I explained how "but" had enough muscles to start a sentence, but only if it were used correctly.

Caution: Do Not Read This Book

Opal sighed and said, "But we just learned this."

I was about to go deeper into how to use a renegade word when I caught myself. Whose words were these, anyway?

As the editor, it was my job to be sure the words flowed, but when did their words become mine?

This book was about students making every decision. Titles were brainstormed, talked about, fretted over and crowd sourced until they agreed on <u>Caution: Do Not Read This Book</u>.

They peppered their passages with "I" and penned passive voices without a whine from me. And they skipped around ideas as if we weren't on a time crunch and secretly threw away the stories they didn't like.

I fished those unloved writes from the trash, smoothed them out and stuck them back into folders with a note, "Love this one! Write some more!" –not unlike Stephen King's wife before his career started.

As a Chief Encourager, I had to remember that these children wrote from limited life experiences. Their ideas were more than that old adage to write what you know; they had to write with the conviction that they were the experts in their lives. Period.

I deleted the "but" and reminded them that I wouldn't change anything unless they were standing there next to me. They asked me to delete an "and" at the beginning of another sentence.

This wasn't an easy project for eight-, nine- and ten-year-old children. Before this publishing class, most viewed first drafts as final drafts and thought you had to rewrite mostly to improve penmanship and readability. With carefully planned lessons, Sharon and I taught them that the game of writing is to make your piece better, then better again.

While editing with a fourth-grader, Manny, I showed him where he wrote three sentences that stated he loved to play in the snow. I told him we needed to

Caution: Do Not Read This Book

remove two of them. Would he cry? He was so proud of writing a long, long, long story.

Without flinching, he pointed to two sentences. Though the writer Hemingway once penned that "You have to kill your darlings" or delete excess words, this was a fourth-grade boy who prized his high word count.

I highlighted the two sentences and said, "OK. This is going to hurt. I'm going to hit the backspace button. These sentences are going away. Ready?"

He nodded fast. "I'm already over these words."

May we all so easily discard our mistakes.

Write. Make it better. Delete. Move on. Write. Make it better. Delete. Move on.

This book is a work of art. And poetry. And might. I hope you love it as much as I do.

Holly Winter
Twitter @mshollywinter

Thank You!

THANK YOU FOR BUYING OUR BOOK. All proceeds of this book will go to the George Washington Montessori school.

Please tell your friends to buy this book.

We're not allowed to talk to strangers, but you can because you're an adult. All adults who are reading this, please tell strangers about this book, too.

You can buy <u>Caution: Do Not Read This Book</u> on Amazon.com.

Made in the USA
Middletown, DE
11 June 2017